PRESENTED TO:

_____

Pray as if everything depends on God,
and work as if everything depends on you.

Francis J. Spellman

PRESENTED BY:

_____

Life's Daily Prayer Book for Teachers
©2004 Elm Hill Books
ISBN: 1-404-18515-1

The quoted ideas expressed in this book (but not Scripture verses) are not, in all cases, exact quotations, as some have been edited for clarity and brevity. In all cases, the author has attempted to maintain the speaker's original intent. In some cases, quoted material for this book was obtained from secondary sources, primarily print media. While every effort has been made to ensure the accuracy of these sources, the accuracy cannot be guaranteed. For additions, deletions, corrections or clarifications in future editions of this text, please write ELM HILL BOOKS.

Manuscript written by Cherie Rayburn in association with Snapdragon Editorial Group, Inc.

LIFE'S *Daily Prayer* BOOK

for Teachers

Prayers to Encourage and Comfort the Soul

Elm Hill Books
An Imprint of J. Countryman®

An old hymn goes: "What a friend we have in Jesus, all our sins and griefs to bear. What a privilege to carry everything to God in prayer." They're wonderful words, aren't they—comforting, strengthening, and liberating. And they are words of truth! In the Bible, God invites us to friendship with Him, a friendship that urges us to cast all our cares on Him.

Life's Daily Prayer Book for Teachers was designed to guide and inspire you as you reach out to God in friendship and converse with Him concerning the issues, activities, and relationships that define your life as a teacher. Think of these written prayers as letters to your best friend—God. Make them your own by adding the names of your students and co-workers and their specific needs. And don't forget to record and date your answers. May God bless you as you embark on this exciting spiritual adventure.

Life's Daily Prayer Book for Teachers
Prayers to Encourage and Comfort the Soul

Fill Thou my life, O Lord my God,
In every part with praise,
That my whole being may proclaim
Thy being and Thy ways.

Horatius Bonar

Daily Prayers of Praise …

*D*aily prayer of praise ...
for Christ's example

*Little children were brought to Him that He
might put His hands on them and pray.*
Matthew 19:13 NKJV

Dear Heavenly Father:

Like most children, the little ones of Jesus' day were probably dirty, noisy, and rambunctious. Your disciples did their best to keep them from disturbing You. And yet You said, "Let them come to Me." You took them in Your arms—runny noses, grimy fingers and all—and You blessed them.

Thank You, Jesus, for Your example. I praise You for showing the world, for all time, how precious children are to You and Your Kingdom. Today, Lord, help me see each of my students through Your eyes, remembering Your gracious example. Let me be a vessel through which Your blessing flows into each of my students.

Amen.

*Jesus said, "Let the children come to me. Don't stop them! For the
Kingdom of Heaven belongs to such as these."*
Matthew 19:14 NLT

MY PERSONAL PRAYER

*Children must be valued as our
most precious possession.*
James Dobson

Dear Father:

_____

_____

_____

_____

_____

_____

_____

Amen

*Jesus said, "Whoever embraces one of these children as I do
embraces me, and far more than me—God who sent me."*
Mark 9:37 MSG

*Jesus said, "Unless you turn from your sins and become as
little children, you will never get into the Kingdom of Heaven."*
Matthew 18:3 NLT

*D*aily prayer of praise …
for each student's uniqueness

The LORD said, "Be glad; rejoice forever in
my creation!"

Isaiah 65:18 NLT

Dear Heavenly Father,

Thank You for Your creativity! Blue eyes, brown eyes, straight hair, curly hair, tall people, short people—the amazing variety of Your creation is evident in the young lives I see every day. I praise You for making each of my students a unique person, an individual not just in outward appearance but also in personality, gifts, strengths, and weaknesses.

Lord, no matter what today brings, help me to remember that each student is precious to You, "fearfully and wonderfully made" in Your very image! Refresh my appreciation of their diversity and renew my wonder in Your awesome creation, so beautifully represented in my students.

Amen.

Body and soul, I am marvelously made! I worship in adoration—
what a creation!
Psalm 139:14 MSG

MY PERSONAL PRAYER

*The potential possibilities of any
child are the most intriguing and
stimulating in all creation.*
Ray L. Wilbur

Dear Father:

_____

_____

_____

_____

_____

_____

Amen

*All of you together are the one body of Christ, and each one
of you is a separate and necessary part of it.*
1 Corinthians 12:27 TLB

*God saw everything that He had made,
and indeed it was very good.*
Genesis 1:31 NKJV

*D*aily prayer of praise ...
for the gift of learning

Guide me in your truth, and teach me, my
God, my Savior. I trust you all day long.
Psalm 25:5 NCV

Dear Heavenly Father,

There's nothing more exciting than seeing a student's
eyes light up when a new concept is grasped or a difficult skill is finally mastered. Unlocking the mysteries of
the world for eager young minds is such a privilege! I
know that all truth is of You, and I praise You for the
opportunity to reveal even the smallest pieces of Your
everlasting truth to my students.

Thank You for the practice of learning, Lord. Today,
show me the best ways to help my students grasp Your
truths about the world. Let me see furrowed brows turn
into smiles of accomplishment as I lead them one step
further along the road of learning.

Amen.

A wise teacher makes learning a joy.
Proverbs 15:2 TLB

MY PERSONAL PRAYER

A teacher affects eternity; he can never tell where his influence stops.
Henry Brooks Adams

Dear Father:

_____

_____

_____

_____

_____

_____

Amen

I have no greater joy than to hear that my children are walking in the truth.
3 John 1:4 NIV

Learning your words gives wisdom and understanding for the foolish.
Psalm 119:130 NCV

Prayer for the Faithful Few

They never stop to make excuse,
but promptly try to do
the very, very best they can
to smooth the way for you.

God bless, I pray, the Faithful Few,
And may their tribe increase;
They must be very precious to
The blessed Prince of Peace!

Author Unknown

Daily Prayers for Special People ...

Daily prayer ...
for my school's leaders

*I exhort first of all that supplications, prayers,
intercessions, and giving of thanks be made for ...
all who are in authority, that we may lead a quiet
and peaceable life in all godliness and reverence.*
1 Timothy 2:1, 2 NKJV

Dear Heavenly Father,

I lift up to You the people You've entrusted with leading our school, particularly the school board members and our principal. Encourage them in the difficult decisions they face on a daily basis. Provide them with Your wisdom, and guide them as they strive to do their very best for the staff members and students they serve.

Lord, help me to be a support, not a hindrance, to these leaders, even when I disagree with their actions and decisions. I know that You have placed them in their positions of leadership. Help me to submit to their authority, give them the benefit of the doubt, and focus on all the good they do.

Amen.

*Remind the believers to be under the authority of rulers and government
leaders, to obey them and be ready to do good.*
Titus 3:1 NCV

MY PERSONAL PRAYER

It is much harder to pray for the leader whose personality is offensive, whose ethics are questionable, who takes the "wrong" position on every issue ... Yet these leaders are also ministers of God ... They do deserve our respect and prayers.

John Eidsmoe

Dear Father:

_____

_____

_____

_____

_____

Amen

Pay to all what is due them ...respect to whom respect is due, honor to whom honor is due.
Romans 13:7 NRSV

Honor those leaders who work so hard for you, who have been given the responsibility of urging and guiding you.
1 Thessalonians 5:12 MSG

Daily prayer …
for my fellow faculty members

Encourage one another and build each other up, just as in fact you are doing.
1 Thessalonians 5:11 NIV

Dear Heavenly Father,

We're all in the same boat—the other teachers and I. And too often, we spend our time together complaining about how rough the sea is or how hard we have to work just to keep things afloat.

Lord, forgive me for those times when I contribute to an atmosphere of negativity in the teacher's lounge. Help me to be a voice of optimism and hope. Show me the good things about being in the teaching "boat," and help me to focus on them in my conversations with others. Thank You for the camaraderie that we share and for bringing us together at this time. Make us a strong team for Your glory!

Amen.

Let your speech always be with grace, seasoned with salt.
Colossians 4:6 NKJV

MY PERSONAL PRAYER

Not only to say the right thing in the right place, but far more difficult to leave unsaid the wrong thing at the tempting moment.

George Sala

Dear Father:

_____

_____

_____

_____

_____

_____

_____

Amen

Walk circumspectly, not as fools but as wise.
Ephesians 5:15 NKJV

You should be like one big happy family, full of sympathy toward each other, loving one another with tender hearts and humble minds.
1 Peter 3:8 TLB

Prayers to Encourage and Comfort the Soul   21

Daily prayer ...
for my school's support staff

*Jesus said, "He who serves you as a servant
is the greatest among you."*
Matthew 23:11 NCV

Dear Heavenly Father,

There are so many people who work behind the scenes
to make our school run smoothly. Their jobs are not
glamorous and are often thankless. Daily, they deal
with some of our school's most challenging situations,
and they do it with cheerfulness and grace.

Lord, thank You for the secretaries, bus drivers,
cafeteria workers, custodians, crossing guards, nurses,
and other support workers without whom our school
literally couldn't function. Thank You for their love of
the students and spirit of servanthood. Make me aware
of opportunities to thank and encourage these special
people for all the things they do to help our school!

Amen.

*The head can't say to the feet, "I don't need you." In fact, some of the
parts that seem weakest and least important are really the most necessary.*
1 Corinthians 12:21, 22 NLT

MY PERSONAL PRAYER

*It is very easy to overestimate
the importance of our own
achievements in comparison with
what we owe others.*

Dietrich Bonhoeffer

Dear Father:

_____

_____

_____

_____

_____

_____

Amen

*I do not cease to give thanks for you as I remember you in
my prayers.*
Ephesians 1:16 NRSV

We belong to each other, and each needs all the others.
Romans 12:5 TLB

*D*aily prayer ...
for my classroom volunteers

> *Do everything you can to help them as well*
> *as all others like them who work hard at your*
> *side with such real devotion.*
>
> 1 Corinthians 16:16 TLB

Dear Heavenly Father,

If I had extra time on my hands, I wonder if I'd use it to chaperone a field trip or help organize a science fair. Thank You, Lord, for those parents and others in our community who step up to the plate time and time again, for those who so generously volunteer their time on behalf our school. They are such a tremendous help to teachers like me who often feel stretched to the limit!

Lord, I pray that You would bless these people as much as they bless us. Give them good experiences and a sense of satisfaction for their efforts. And never let me forget to express my sincere appreciation to them.

Amen.

With thankful hearts, offer up your prayers and requests to God.
Philippians 4:6 CEV

MY PERSONAL PRAYER

Appreciation is a wonderful thing:
it makes what is excellent in others
belong to us as well.

François de Voltaire

Dear Father:

_____

_____

_____

_____

_____

_____

Amen

Whatever good anyone does, he will receive
the same from the Lord.
Ephesians 6:8 NKJV

When we have the opportunity to help anyone, we should do it.
Galatians 6:10 NCV

*D*aily prayer ...
for my students' parents

*Hear, my child, your father's instruction, and
do not reject your mother's teaching.*

Proverbs 1:8 NRSV

Dear Heavenly Father,

Sometimes I forget that I'm not the only teacher in
my students' lives. There are moms and dads whose
influence came long before mine and will last long
after my class has ended.

Lord, I pray for my students' parents. Give them Your
wisdom in the world's most important job—raising a
child. Help them know how to provide the kind of
support and encouragement that their children need to
succeed scholastically, and help them see the importance
of being involved in their children's school experience.

Lord, may You allow a strong partnership to exist
between my students' parents and me, and together,
may we do all we can to ensure that their children
grow into healthy, happy, and responsible adults.

Amen.

*Now a word to you parents ...Bring [your children] up with the loving
discipline the Lord himself approves, with suggestions and godly advice.*
Ephesians 6:4 TLB

MY PERSONAL PRAYER

*What greater work is there than
training the mind and forming the
habits of the young?*
Saint John Chrysostom

Dear Father:

_____

_____

_____

_____

_____

_____

Amen

*Train a child how to live the right way. Then even when
he is old, he will still live that way.*
Proverbs 22:6 NCV

*Discipline your children; you'll be glad you did—
they'll turn out delightful to live with.*
Proverbs 29:17 MSG

Prayers to Encourage and Comfort the Soul　　　27

*D*aily prayer ...
for the first-year teacher

The Lord GOD has given me the tongue of
the learned, that I should know how to speak
a word in season to him who is weary.

Isaiah 50:4 NKJV

Dear Heavenly Father,

It seems like just yesterday that I walked into "my very own classroom" for the first time. The feelings I had were a jumble of anticipation, anxiety, excitement, and—most of all—fear.

Lord, help me to remember how I felt, the questions I had, and the special guidance I needed during my first year as a teacher. Then give me the sensitivity to reach out to the first-year teachers in my school. Give me the right words to say at the right times, words that will encourage the hearts of these special young people and make the most difficult year of their career—the first year—a little easier and more rewarding.

Amen.

If your gift is to encourage others, do it! ... And if you have a gift for
showing kindness to others, do it gladly.

Romans 12:8 NLT

MY PERSONAL PRAYER

We must support one another, console one another, mutually help, counsel, and advise.

Thomas à Kempis

Dear Father:

_____

_____

_____

_____

_____

_____

Amen

Jesus said, "Ask yourself what you want people to do for you, then grab the initiative and do it for them."
Matthew 7:12 MSG

Speak encouragement.
1 Kings 22:13 NKJV

Daily prayer ...

for our substitute teachers

The godly people in the land are my true heroes! I take pleasure in them!

Psalm 16:3 NLT

Dear Heavenly Father,

In this life there are few heroes to look up to. Truly, substitute teachers are some of the most heroic people I know! Thank You for those substitutes who fearlessly tackle classes that think a day with a substitute is a day of play. Thank You for their dedication, patience, and willingness to step into the middle of things without any preparation.

Lord, help me teach my students to respect a substitute teacher as they would me. I want my classes to be every substitute's dream—not a nightmare! And remind me to take every opportunity to express my sincere appreciation to our school's faithful substitutes.

Amen.

Do the hard work of getting along with each other, treating each other with dignity and honor.

James 3:18 MSG

MY PERSONAL PRAYER

I am only one, but still I am one; I cannot do everything, but still I can do something; and because I cannot do everything, I will not refuse to do the something that I can do.

Edward Everett Hale

Dear Father:

_____

_____

_____

_____

_____

_____

Amen

Be ready in season and out of season.
2 Timothy 4:2 NASB

Surely you will reward each person according to what he has done.
Psalm 62:12 NIV

My Daily Prayer

If I can do some good today,
If I can serve along life's way,
If I can something helpful say,
Lord, show me how.

If I can right a human wrong,
If I can help to make one strong,
If I can cheer with smile or song,
Lord, show me how.

If I can aid one in distress,
If I can make a burden less,
If I can spread more happiness,
Lord, show me how.

Grenville Kleiser

Daily Prayers for My Students ...

Daily prayer …
for the perfectionist student

We who are strong in faith should help the
weak with their weaknesses.

Romans 15:1 NCV

Dear Heavenly Father,

Often, I get so caught up in dealing with the difficult
students in my class that I forget other students who
need just as much attention—perfectionist students.
You know whom they are, Lord, the ones who feel like
they have failed if they make an A rather than an A+
or 95 rather than 100.

Lord, make me sensitive to these students' very real
anxiety and show me how to help them lighten up on
their expectations of themselves. I pray that You would
help me emphasize the joy of learning over earning
good grades. And remind me to praise all my students
for whom they are, not just for how they perform.

Amen.

Let God transform you inwardly … Then you will be able to know the
will of God—what is good and is pleasing to him and is perfect.
Romans 12:2 GNT

MY PERSONAL PRAYER

You must look into people,
as well as at them.

Lord Chesterfield

Dear Father:

_____

_____

_____

_____

_____

_____

Amen

There is now no condemnation
for those who are in Christ Jesus.
Romans 8:1 NASB

Jesus said, "The work that I ask you to accept is easy.
The load I give you to carry is not heavy."
Matthew 11:30 NCV

aily prayer ...
for the unmotivated student

Be patient with every person.
1 Thessalonians 5:14 NCV

Dear Heavenly Father,

What does it take? Lord, I've racked my brain over that question so often. What does it take to get an unmotivated student to want to succeed? I've used everything from bribes to threats, and still, some students refuse to even try.

Lord, if I have missed something, some secret motivational key that will reach these students, please make me aware of what that is. And if there is truly nothing else I can do, please help me to let go. Help me to entrust these students to You, knowing that You have the power to change even the most reluctant student into an eager learner.

Amen.

If you want to know what God wants you to do,
ask him, and He will gladly tell you.
James 1:5 TLB

MY PERSONAL PRAYER

*To attain positive results,
be positive.*

Author Unknown

Dear Father:

_____

_____

_____

_____

_____

_____

_____

Amen

*In him all the treasures of wisdom and
knowledge are safely kept.*
Colossians 2:3 NCV

*Jesus said, "The people I love, I call to account—prod and
correct and guide so that they'll live at their best."*
Revelation 3:19 MSG

*D*aily prayer ...

for the foreign student

> *God says, "Do not take advantage of foreign-*
> *ers in your land ... love them as yourself."*
> Leviticus 19:33, 34 TLB

Dear Heavenly Father,

I love the fact that our country is like a colorful, patch-work quilt made up of people from every corner of the world. But I have a hard time being excited when a new piece of the quilt ends up in my classroom. It's often frustrating to deal with my regular class, plus a student who has difficulty speaking English and a different way of doing even the littlest things.

Lord, give me an extra measure of patience with my foreign-born students. Help me to appreciate their differences. Show me how to make them feel at home and to integrate them as a beautiful and important piece in the "quilt" of my class.

Amen.

> *Do not forget to entertain strangers,*
> *for by so doing some have unwittingly entertained angels.*
> Hebrews 13:2 NKJV

MY PERSONAL PRAYER

If a man be gracious and courteous to strangers, it shows he is a citizen of the world.

Francis Bacon

Dear Father:

_____

_____

_____

_____

_____

_____

Amen

Love is patient and kind. Love is not ... boastful or proud or rude. Love does not demand its own way. Love is not irritable.
1 Corinthians 13:4, 5 NLT

The LORD says, "If you do not oppress the alien ... then I will dwell with you in this place."
Jeremiah 7:6, 7 NRSV

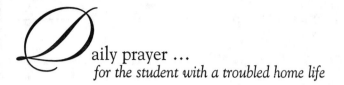
aily prayer …
for the student with a troubled home life

> *"Comfort, comfort my people,"*
> *says your God.*
>
> Isaiah 40:1 NLT

Dear Heavenly Father,

How I wish that each of my students came from a perfect home where harmony and love reign. It breaks my heart to see students suffer because of things happening at home that are beyond their control. It's hard to believe the old notion that "kids are resilient" when their eyes are brimming with tears and they are too distracted by emotional pain to pay attention in class.

Lord, for these hurting students I pray an outpouring of Your love, mercy, and grace. Help me know when to offer them words of consolation and when just to listen. And please surround them with Your angels of comfort and peace—especially at home.

Thank You, Lord, for loving these students even more than I do.

Amen.

God comforts us in all our troubles so that we can comfort others.
2 Corinthians 1:4 NLT

MY PERSONAL PRAYER

*God does not comfort us
to make us comfortable,
but to make us comforters.*

John Henry Jowett

Dear Father:

_____

_____

_____

_____

_____

_____

Amen

Jesus said, "In this godless world you will continue to experience difficulties. But take heart! I've conquered the world."
John 16:33 MSG

*Jesus said, "Blessed are those who mourn,
for they shall be comforted."*
Matthew 5:4 NKJV

*D*aily prayer ...

for the gifted student

> *They will be radiant because of the many
> gifts the LORD has given them.*
> Jeremiah 31:12 NLT

Dear Heavenly Father,

My gifted students are such a joy. Thank You for their quick minds and boundless desire to learn. Guide me, Lord, in providing them learning challenges that will stretch their knowledge and skills. And on those occasions when they progress beyond even me, help me to be genuinely excited for them, ever encouraging them forward.

Lord, most importantly, help me steer my gifted students away from a common pitfall of the very bright—pride and arrogance. Give me the words and actions that will instill in these students a gratitude for their giftedness and a sense of compassion that will focus their exceptional abilities on doing good for others.

Amen.

> *An excellent spirit, knowledge, and understanding to interpret dreams,
> explain riddles, and solve problems were found in ... Daniel.*
> Daniel 5:12 NRSV

MY PERSONAL PRAYER

When love and skill work together,
expect a masterpiece.

John Ruskin

Dear Father:

_____

_____

_____

_____

_____

_____

Amen

Jesus said, "To one he gave five talents, to another, two, and
to another, one, each according to his own ability."
Matthew 25:15 NASB

Having then gifts differing according to the grace that is given
to us, let us use them.
Romans 12:6 NKJV

*D*aily prayer ...

for the slow learner

Comfort the feebleminded, support the weak,
be patient toward all.

1 Thessalonians 5:14 KJV

Dear Heavenly Father,

I get so impatient when I'm dealing with slow learners—impatient with myself! I want desperately to make a difference in their lives, to help them succeed at learning. That's why I went into teaching, after all. But with these students, I often feel like I'm trying to go up on a down escalator.

Lord, give me a double measure of Your patience to deal effectively with my slow learners. Help me to celebrate even the smallest steps forward and not be discouraged when I feel like I'm just treading water. Most importantly, Lord, I pray that through me, You would show these special students how valuable they are, despite their learning disadvantages.

Amen.

You must support the weak.
Acts 20:35 NKJV

MY PERSONAL PRAYER

The times we find ourselves having to wait on others may be the perfect opportunities to train ourselves to wait on the Lord.

Joni Eareckson Tada

Dear Father:

_____

_____

_____

_____

_____

_____

Amen

The servant of the Lord must not strive; but be gentle unto all men, apt to teach, patient.
2 Timothy 2:24 KJV

Jesus said, "The Helper will teach you everything. He will cause you to remember all the things I told you. This Helper is the Holy Spirit whom the Father will send in my name."
John 14:26 NCV

Prayers to Encourage and Comfort the Soul

45

‍‌Daily prayer …

for the rejected student

> *By [the glory of His grace] God made us*
> *accepted in the Beloved.*
>
> Ephesians 1:6 NKJV

Dear Heavenly Father,

I love my students, but sometimes they can be so mean and insensitive, particularly to those who don't quite fit in. Lord, I hurt for those students the others reject, those who have to eat lunch by themselves and are never chosen for group projects.

I know that You have a special love for the rejected. During Your time on earth, You embraced all kinds of outcasts—prostitutes, tax collectors, and lepers. Thank You for also embracing the rejected students in our school, for seeing the tremendous potential in them. Help me, Lord, to make my classroom a safe place for them, a place where all students are accepted and loved, just the way they are.

Amen.

> *Accept one another, then, just as Christ accepted you,*
> *in order to bring praise to God.*
>
> Romans 15:7 NIV

MY PERSONAL PRAYER

*No soul is desolate as long as there
is a human being for whom it can
feel trust and reverence.*

George Eliot

Dear Father:

_____

_____

_____

_____

_____

_____

Amen

*Jesus was rejected by the people,
but he is precious to God who chose Him.*
1 Peter 2:4 NLT

*God sets on high those who are lowly,
and those who mourn are lifted to safety.*
Job 5:11 NKJV

$\mathcal{D}$aily prayer ...

for the new student

Welcome him in the Lord with great joy.
Philippians 2:29 NIV

Dear Heavenly Father,

I don't think anything is more frightening than being "the new kid," particularly in the middle of the school year. Lord, give me a warm and welcoming spirit for the new students assigned to my class, even when I'm feeling that my classroom is already overcrowded.

Let me anticipate when to provide special attention to help them adjust quickly to our school's rules and schedules. Help our new students to feel "at home" in our school, and encourage the other students to be kind and willing to take them into their circle of friends. Give us all a special sensitivity for these students, reminding us what it's like to be new and lonely.

Amen.

Be inventive in hospitality.
Romans 12:13 MSG

MY PERSONAL PRAYER

*He who makes room in his heart
for others, will himself find accom-
modation everywhere.*

Author Unknown

Dear Father:

_____

_____

_____

_____

_____

_____

_____

Amen

Extend every hospitality.
1 Kings 2:7 MSG

*Jesus said, "Whoever welcomes this little child in my name
welcomes me; and whoever welcomes me welcomes the one
who sent me."*
Luke 9:48 NIV

Prayers to Encourage and Comfort the Soul   49

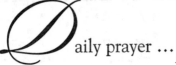

*D*aily prayer ...

for the troubled student

To discipline and reprimand a child produces
wisdom.

Proverbs 29:15 NLT

Dear Heavenly Father,

Do I sound like a broken record to You? It seems that every day I'm saying the same things over and over to the same students—"Stop that. Put that back. Sit down. Be quiet." Sometimes I wonder if the thorn in the apostle Paul's side wasn't a student with a discipline problem!

Lord, help me get through to students who are perpetually a "thorn" in my side! Give me the patience not to react in anger when they disrupt my class. And help me implement effective teaching methods that will encourage them to adopt appropriate behaviors. Above all, Lord, keep my relationship with these students positive, no matter how many times a day I have to correct them.

Amen.

Sound advice is a beacon, good teaching is a light,
moral discipline is a life path.
Proverbs 6:23 MSG

MY PERSONAL PRAYER

Discipline is the rudimentary thread of the learning cloak.
Author Unknown

Dear Father:

_____

_____

_____

_____

_____

_____

Amen

*If you love your children, you will be prompt
to discipline them.*
Proverbs 13:24 NLT

*Discipline your children while you still have the chance;
indulging them destroys them.*
Proverbs 19:18 MSG

*D*aily prayer ...

for the student I dislike

God shows personal favoritism to no man.
Galatians 2:6 NKJV

Dear Heavenly Father,

Occasionally there's a student that I simply don't like. It's hard to put my finger on the reason why, but I guess our personalities just clash. Lord, I know that all my students are precious in Your sight, that You love them all equally, without any discrimination.

Let me see my students through Your eyes, and impress on my heart the good in each of them. Never let me play favorites or treat any of my students unfairly just because I don't happen to prefer them. Thank You, Lord, for loving me even when I'm unlovable—help me to love my students in the same way.

Amen.

*The wisdom that comes from heaven is first of all pure;
then peace-loving, considerate, submissive, full of mercy and
good fruit, impartial and sincere.*
James 3:17 NIV

MY PERSONAL PRAYER

Love's business is not to play
favorites. It is no respecter
of persons.

Joseph Fletcher

Dear Father:

_____

_____

_____

_____

_____

_____

Amen

I charge you, in the sight of God and Christ Jesus and the
elect angels ... to do nothing out of favoritism.
1 Timothy 5:21 NIV

To show partiality is not good.
Proverbs 28:21 NIV

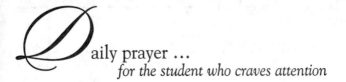

Daily prayer ...
for the student who craves attention

*Mercy to the needy is a loan to God, and
God pays back those loans in full.*

Proverbs 19:17 MSG

Dear Heavenly Father,

I offer a special prayer for my needy students. Not those who need material things, but those who need attention ... lots and lots of attention. Lord, these students are like wind-up toys. Their efforts to be in the middle of everything go on and on.

Lord, I often find myself getting annoyed at these students and, sometimes, venting my frustration on them. Help me to understand how emotionally needy and insecure they are. Help me to give them the kind of unconditional love that will build them up, making them more secure in themselves and calming their craving for attention.

Amen.

God will help the needy when no one else will help.
Psalm 72:12 NCV

MY PERSONAL PRAYER

*Christianity demands a level
of caring that transcends
human inclinations.*

Erwin W. Lutzer

Dear Father:

_____

_____

_____

_____

_____

_____

Amen

The LORD hears the cries of his needy ones.
Psalm 69:33 NLT

*I bow my knees to the Father ... that you, being rooted and
grounded in love, may be able to comprehend with all the
saints what is the width and length and depth and height—to
know the love of Christ which passes knowledge.*
Ephesians 3:14, 17–19 NKJV

Prayer for the Day

Lord, may I enter this day without hurry;
May I bear its burdens without complaint.
May I face its tasks without fear.
May I meet its temptations without dishon-
or.
May I rest at its close without shame.
And this prayer I make to Thee,
Let Thy kingdom come today in me.

Author Unknown

Daily Prayers for Special Days
and Events ...

Daily prayer ...

for the first day of school

> *Let us therefore come boldly unto the throne*
> *of grace, that we may obtain mercy, and find*
> *grace to help in time of need.*
>
> Hebrews 4:16 KJV

Dear Heavenly Father,

Every year, I approach the first day of school with both apprehension and eagerness. No matter how much time I've spent preparing, no matter how many successful years I have under my belt, the first day of school is always an anxious one for me.

Lord, today, and every day of the coming school year, I claim Your promise to always be with me and never to forsake me. Let Your presence and love fill every corner of my classroom, and may the year ahead be filled with many stories of joy and success.

Amen.

In the morning, I lay my requests before you and wait in expectation.
Psalm 5:3 NIV

MY PERSONAL PRAYER

Every September is like Christmas,
and every student,
a surprise gift to open.
Mary Vissilikou Bicouvaris, 1989
U.S. Teacher of the Year

Dear Father:

_____

_____

_____

_____

_____

_____

Amen

Behold, I am doing a new thing; now it springs forth,
do you not perceive it?
Isaiah 43:19 RSV

This is the day the LORD has made;
we will rejoice and be glad in it.
Psalm 118:24 NKJV

Prayers to Encourage and Comfort the Soul   59

*D*aily prayer ...

for parent conferences

> *Don't fret or worry. Instead of worrying,*
> *pray. Let petitions and praises shape your*
> *worries into prayers, letting God know your*
> *concerns.*
>
> Philippians 4:6 MSG

Dear Heavenly Father,

My students' parents are just as varied as my students! Some of them are sweet and understanding, others are brusque and contentious, and still others are bored and apathetic. I always look forward to my conferences with them with fear and trembling.

Lord, help me to remember that parent conferences are not about me—they're about my students. They're about forging a partnership with my students' parents that will provide the very best circumstances for my students to grow. Help me approach parent conferences with a positive attitude. Give me the right words to say to build each parent's confidence in me.

Amen.

> *Be not afraid of their faces: for I am with thee.*
> Jeremiah 1:8 KJV

MY PERSONAL PRAYER

*God has not called me to be
successful; he has called
me to be faithful.*

Mother Teresa

Dear Father:

_____

_____

_____

_____

_____

_____

Amen

*You, O LORD, will bless the righteous; With favor You will
surround him as with a shield.*
Psalm 5:12 NKJV

Work together in peace.
Zechariah 6:13 NCV

$\mathscr{D}$aily prayer ...

for teacher workshops

> *Above all and before all, do this: Get*
> *Wisdom! Write this at the top of your list:*
> *Get Understanding!*
>
> Proverbs 4:7 MSG

Dear Heavenly Father,

Teachers are notorious for being know-it-alls. Lord, please don't ever let me get to the point where I believe I know everything about teaching and have nothing new to learn. Let me approach each opportunity to learn something new with an open mind and heart.

I especially pray for the workshops that our school's and district's leaders put so much effort into providing for us. Let each workshop I attend provide new information that I can use to do a better job. Let me look forward to these valuable opportunities to learn and become a more competent teacher—for my students' sake.

Amen.

A wise man will hear, and will increase learning; and a man of under-
standing shall attain unto wise counsels.

Proverbs 1:5 KJV

MY PERSONAL PRAYER

There is always a better way …
your challenge is to find it.
Author Unknown

Dear Father:

_____

_____

_____

_____

_____

_____

Amen

Teach me good judgment and knowledge.
Psalm 119:66 NLT

Give instruction to a wise man, and he will be yet wiser:
teach a just man, and he will increase in learning.
Proverbs 9:9 KJV

*D*aily prayer ...
for field trips

> *He orders his angels to protect you wherever*
> *you go. They will hold you with their hands.*
> Psalm 91:11, 12 NLT

Dear Heavenly Father,

It's a sad fact: Everybody looks forward to a field trip—
except the teacher in charge. Keeping kids together,
safe, and out of trouble on a field trip is such a huge
responsibility!

Lord, I remember how important field trips were when
I was a student. They made a huge impression on my
life and produced some of my favorite memories. Help
me provide memory-making experiences for my students on field trips. Keep them safe, and open their
eyes to the wonders of the world outside our classroom.
And please, help me to relax and enjoy the experience
with them.

Amen.

> *Trust in God at all times.*
> Psalm 62:8 KJV

MY PERSONAL PRAYER

The mediocre teacher tells.
The good teacher explains.
The superior teacher demonstrates.
The great teacher inspires.
William Arthur Ward

Dear Father:

_____

_____

_____

_____

_____

_____

Amen

If you are a teacher, do a good job of teaching.
Romans 12:7 TLB

Teach the wise, and they will be wiser. Teach the righteous,
and they will learn more.
Proverbs 9:9 NLT

Daily prayer ...

for open house

Dear Heavenly Father,

I love Open House. It's an evening when my students and I have the chance to "show off" for some very important people—their parents. I also dread Open House. I want everything to be perfect. I want each parent who attends to be impressed not just with my classroom but also with me.

Lord, take away my Open House insecurities. Give me the confidence that my dedication to teaching and to my students will be evident to the parents. And as we meet for the first time, let us make positive connections—connections that will grow throughout the year into solid alliances dedicated to the success and happiness of the young lives in our care.

Amen.

MY PERSONAL PRAYER

Humility is the greatest expression of confidence.

Author Unknown

Dear Father:

_____

_____

_____

_____

_____

_____

Amen

Is not your reverence your confidence? And the integrity of your ways your hope?
Job 4:6 NKJV

We are confident of all this because of our great trust in God through Christ.
2 Corinthians 3:4 NLT

$\mathcal{D}$aily prayer ...
for holiday celebrations

Dear Heavenly Father,

Thank You for the sparkle in my students' eyes and the excitement in their voices as they look forward to holidays. No matter how many homemade valentines or paper Thanksgiving turkeys decorate my room year after year, I'm always amazed at the creativity and imagination that holidays inspire in young minds.

Holidays and children were made for each other, and when these special days come along, I feel especially fortunate to be a teacher, because I get to see them through the eyes of my students. Lord, help me to make holidays memorable times in my classroom, and let them be happy occasions in each of my students' homes too.

Amen.

Live creatively, friends.
Galatians 6:1 MSG

MY PERSONAL PRAYER

*God is our Creator. God made us
in his image and likeness.
Therefore we are creators ... The
joy of creativeness should be ours.*
Dorothy May Day

Dear Father:

_____

_____

_____

_____

_____

_____

Amen

*Come to the joyous celebrations ...
For God has given us these times of joy.*
Psalm 81:3, 4 TLB

*Accept our praise, O Lord, for all your glorious power.
We will write songs to celebrate your mighty acts!*
Psalm 21:13 TLB

Prayers to Encourage and Comfort the Soul   69

*D*aily prayer ...

for fire drills

> *The LORD says, "Do not fear, for I am with you; Do not anxiously look about you, for I am your God. I will strengthen you, surely I will help you."*
>
> Isaiah 41:10 NASB

Dear Heavenly Father,

I remember fire drills when I was young. There was an element of suspense in not knowing when they would occur, and the prospect of getting to go outside when it wasn't even recess was always exciting.

Lord, since 9/11, fire and other emergency preparedness drills have a whole new tone. They are so much more serious now, and it is so much more important that my class understands their seriousness. Lord, help me be able to impress on my students the importance of following drill instructions, without making them overly anxious. And I pray that in the event of a true emergency, You would hold us all in Your protective, loving arms.

Amen.

> *What joy for all who find protection in him!*
> Psalm 2:12 NLT

MY PERSONAL PRAYER

With responsibility comes great burden. With the acceptance of this load comes newfound strength.
Author Unknown

Dear Father:

_____

_____

_____

_____

_____

_____

Amen

Don't be afraid … do not dread those things.
Isaiah 8:12 NCV

Perfect love casts out fear, because fear involves torment. But he who fears has not been made perfect in love.
1 John 4:18 NKJV

*D*aily prayer ...

for class programs

> *God hath not given us the spirit of fear; but*
> *of power, and of love, and of a sound mind.*
> 2 Timothy 1:7 KJV

Dear Heavenly Father,

Nothing is more exciting than the day of a class program. I love the feel of anticipation in the air as students stand nervously backstage, waiting for the curtain to rise.

Lord, I pray that my students will have great memories of their class programs. Help them to remember their lines and not be overcome by stage fright. Let each audience be welcoming and enthusiastic, and let my students be proud of their performance. Don't let any mistakes they make discourage them, and help me to have realistic expectations. Let my students enjoy being in the spotlight and the well-deserved applause that their hard work brings!

Amen.

> *Say to them that are of a fearful heart, Be strong, fear not.*
> Isaiah 35:4 KJV

MY PERSONAL PRAYER   *No matter how small, acknowledge*
the achievement.
Author Unknown

Dear Father:

_____

_____

_____

_____

_____

_____

_____

Amen

You are my joy and the reward for my work.
Philippians 4:1 NLT

Behold, His reward is with Him.
Isaiah 40:10 NKJV

*D*aily prayer ...

The LORD your God says, "I will give you
rain in its season."
Leviticus 26:4 NKJV

Dear Heavenly Father,

This is a special prayer for those days when the weather is gloomy and everyone in my class is grumpy—including me! Something about a rainy day always dampens everyone's spirit, and when there are several days in a row with "indoor recess," nerves get frayed and the learning process suffers.

Lord, help me to be prepared for rainy days, both in my lesson plans and my attitude. I know that I set the tone for my class, and if a gloomy day gets me down, it will get my students down too. Help me find ways to make even rainy days exciting, filled with interesting learning opportunities that make them go by quickly.

Amen.

The intelligent man is always open to new ideas.
In fact, he looks for them.
Proverbs 18:15 TLB

MY PERSONAL PRAYER

You can think, talk, and act your-self into dullness or into monotony or into unhappiness. By the same process you can build up inspira-tion, excitement, and a surging depth of joy.

Dear Father:

Norman Vincent Peale

_____

_____

_____

_____

_____

_____

Amen

Rejoice in the Lord always: and again I say, Rejoice.
Philippians 4:4 KJV

The Lord will open up his storehouse. The skies will send rain on your land at the right time.
Deuteronomy 28:12 NCV

$\mathcal{D}$aily prayer ...
for the last day of school

"I am Alpha and Omega, the Beginning and the End," says the Lord.
Revelation 1:8 NKJV

Dear Heavenly Father,

It's finally here ... the day I've been looking forward to since school started! So why do I have such mixed emotions now? Pride in my class's accomplishments is tangled up with questions like "Did I miss anything important? Are my students really prepared for what they'll encounter next year? Did I do a good job?"

Lord, it's time for me to place each of these precious lives in Your hands. Watch over them this summer, and bless them as they go forward. I pray that everything they've learned and experienced this past year will be a positive step toward their becoming everything they're meant to be. Thank You for letting me be part of their lives!

Amen.

Give all your worries to him, because he cares for you.
1 Peter 5:7 NCV

MY PERSONAL PRAYER   *Every end is a new beginning.*
                                    Robert Harold Schuller

Dear Father:

_____

_____

_____

_____

_____

_____

                                          Amen

*Being confident of this, that he who began a good work in you
will carry it on to completion until the day of Christ Jesus.*
Philippians 1:6 NIV

Better is the end of a thing than the beginning thereof.
Ecclesiastes 7:8 KJV

A Prayer of Affirmation

I rise today with the power of
God to guide me,
the might of God to uphold me,
the wisdom of God to teach me,
the eye of God to watch over me,
the ear of God to hear me,
the word of God to give me speech,
the hand of God to protect me,
the path of God to lie before me,
the shield of God to shelter me,
the host of God to defend me.

Saint Patrick

Daily Prayers for Guidance
and Wisdom ...

Daily prayer for guidance and wisdom …
when I'm preparing lesson plans

Let God tell you what to do;
take his words to heart.

Job 22:22 MSG

Dear Heavenly Father,

It seems there are a million teaching methods out there, each one claiming to be better than all the rest. Lord, help me as I consider how to communicate the skills and concepts that my students need to learn. Show me the most effective ways to reach them.

Lord, don't ever let me get so "stuck" on a particular teaching method that I forget to consider, first and foremost, my students' varied learning styles. Make me flexible and willing to abandon even my favorite methods if need be. Keep me humble and ever aware that it's not about me—it's about doing what it takes to equip my students to succeed at school and life.

Amen.

Depend on the Lord in whatever you do. Then your plans will succeed.
Proverbs 16:3 NCV

MY PERSONAL PRAYER

God has led. God will lead.
God is leading!
Richard C. Halverson

Dear Father:

_____

_____

_____

_____

_____

_____

Amen

People can make many different plans.
But only the Lord's plan will happen.
Proverbs 19:21 NCV

Plans succeed through good counsel.
Proverbs 20:18 NLT

aily prayer for
guidance and wisdom ...
when I disagree with the curriculum

> For the Lord's sake accept the authority of
> every human institution.
>
> 1 Peter 2:13 NRSV

Dear Heavenly Father,

I don't like the curriculum that's been chosen for my class. I wish I could just throw it out the window and start from scratch, but I know I would be in big trouble if I did that!

Lord, show me the good things about this curriculum. Show me what will meet my students' learning needs and nurture their unique gifts. Then, show me how to fill in the gaps. Give me the creativity and wisdom to know how best to make up for this curriculum's deficits. And help me not to be critical of the curriculum decision makers but to provide constructive input that will help them make better choices in the future.

Amen.

> *Each of you must take responsibility for doing the creative best you can.*
> Galatians 6:5 MSG

MY PERSONAL PRAYER

*Opportunities multiply
as they are seized.*
Author Unknown

Dear Father:

_____

_____

_____

_____

_____

_____

Amen

Insight and strength are mine.
Proverbs 8:14 NLT

*Servants, you must respect your masters
and do whatever they tell you.*
1 Peter 2:18 TLB

*D*aily prayer for
guidance and wisdom ...
when I have limited supplies

> *God is able to provide you with every blessing*
> *in abundance, so that you may always have*
> *enough of everything and may provide in*
> *abundance for every good work.*
>
> 2 Corinthians 9:8 RSV

Dear Heavenly Father,

There's so much I want to teach my students, so much I want them to experience! But too often, I feel held back by the lack of supplies, and I can't afford to keep spending my own money for them.

Lord, I know Your Word says that You provide everything Your children need. Teach me to trust in Your provision for me and my class. I know that You want my students to learn all that they can even more than I do. Now help me to relax in that knowledge and to trust that for those times when supplies are short, You will either provide them or show me how to be effective without them.

Amen.

> *My God shall supply all your need according to his riches*
> *in glory by Christ Jesus.*
>
> Philippians 4:19 KJV

MY PERSONAL PRAYER

Real leaders are ordinary people with extraordinary determination.
Author Unknown

Dear Father:

_____

_____

_____

_____

_____

_____

Amen

I will abundantly bless [Zion's] provision.
Psalm 132:15 NKJV

Everyone's needs will be met.
2 Corinthians 8:14 NLT

aily prayer for
guidance and wisdom ...
when I fall behind

> *From the end of the earth I will cry to You,*
> *When my heart is overwhelmed; Lead me to*
> *the rock that is higher than I.*
>
> Psalm 61:2 NKJV

Dear Heavenly Father,

I can barely see over the pile on my desk, and I'm beginning to feel overwhelmed! Every task needs urgent attention, but there are only so many hours in a day.

Lord, I know You created each day with twenty-four hours, and I know that if I'm living my life in harmony with Your will, that's enough time to accomplish everything You have for me to do. Help me know which commitments in my overcrowded life to give up, and help me to prioritize the rest. Help me get caught up on the things that are truly in Your will for me to do, and let me seek You every morning to bring order and balance into my day.

Amen.

> *Jesus said, "Do not be anxious about tomorrow, for tomorrow will be*
> *anxious for itself. Let the day's own trouble be sufficient for the day."*
> Matthew 6:34 RSV

MY PERSONAL PRAYER

*How do you eat an elephant?
One bite at a time.*

Author Unknown

Dear Father:

_____

_____

_____

_____

_____

_____

Amen

*I will bless the Lord who counsels me; he gives me wisdom
in the night. He tells me what to do.*
Psalm 16:7 TLB

*They that wait upon the LORD shall renew their strength;
they shall mount up with wings as eagles; they shall run, and
not be weary; and they shall walk, and not faint.*
Isaiah 40:31 KJV

*D*aily prayer for
guidance and wisdom ...
when I'm determining grades

*Light shines on those who do right. Joy
belongs to those who are honest. Rejoice in the
Lord, you who do right. Praise his holy name.*

Psalm 97:11, 12 NCV

Dear Heavenly Father,

Assigning grades is definitely the best and worst of
times. I love recording a good grade for a student who
has worked hard and earned it. I hate recording a bad
grade for a student who has performed poorly, especially
when I know I'll get a phone call from an angry parent.

Lord, I know my job in assigning grades is to tell the
truth in love, however painful for me or the student.
Please give me the courage to always be honest and fair
in assessing students' performances. Don't let me suc-
cumb to the temptation to "fudge" even a little bit.
And give me the wisdom and sensitivity to help those
students whose performance is suffering.

Amen.

*Good people will be happy in the Lord. They will find protection in him.
Let everyone who is honest praise the Lord.*

Psalm 64:10 NCV

MY PERSONAL PRAYER

Truth cannot fly without love, nor can love soar aloft without truth.

Ephraem the Syrian

Dear Father:

_____

_____

_____

_____

_____

_____

Amen

We will hold to the truth in love, becoming more and more in every way like Christ.
Ephesians 4:15 NLT

*The wisdom that comes from God ...
is always fair and honest.*
James 3:17 NCV

*D*aily prayer for
guidance and wisdom ...
when I need someone to talk to

*Plans fail without good advice, but plans suc-
ceed when you get advice from many others.*
Proverbs 15:22 NCV

Dear Heavenly Father,

Sometimes it seems that no one understands me, not
even my family and friends. There are just some things
only another teacher can relate to!

Lord, I pray that You would keep mentors in my life—
Christian teachers who are more experienced than I
and who are willing to spend some one-on-one time
with me. Help me to share openly with them about my
frustrations and failures, and give them the words of
encouragement and advice I need to hear. Also make
me aware of younger teachers I might need to mentor,
and help me to be a positive, empathetic influence in
their lives.

Amen.

Hold tight to good advice; don't relax your grip. Guard it well.
Proverbs 4:13 MSG

MY PERSONAL PRAYER   *The teacher who loves to learn is*
an exciting teacher.
Greg Henry Quinn

Dear Father:

_____

_____

_____

_____

_____

_____

Amen

The godly give good advice, but fools are destroyed by their
lack of common sense.
Proverbs 10:21 NLT

Though good advice lies deep within a counselor's heart,
the wise man will draw it out.
Proverbs 20:5 TLB

Prayers to Encourage and Comfort the Soul   91

*D*aily prayer for
guidance and wisdom …
when my classroom is disorganized

Lead them by your good example.
1 Peter 5:3 NLT

Dear Heavenly Father,

It looks like a tornado hit my classroom. I'd be really embarrassed if a parent walked in right now. I know that a chaotic environment is not conducive to learning, but I'm just too exhausted to do anything about it.

Lord, it's so easy to let little messes go until they become big ones. Help me to be aware of, and attend to, the little messes before they grow out of control. Let me be a good example of order and tidiness to my students, and help me to learn effective strategies for staying on top of even those mundane "housekeeping" chores in my classroom.

Amen.

An orderly way of life can be maintained.
Romans 13:6 MSG

MY PERSONAL PRAYER

Have a time and place for every-thing, and do everything in its time and place, and you will not only accomplish more, but have far more leisure than those who are always hurrying.

Tryon Edwards

Dear Father:

_____

_____

_____

_____

_____

_____

Amen

I am delighted to hear of the careful and orderly ways you conduct your affairs.
Colossians 2:5 MSG

You should do good deeds to be an example in every way.
Titus 2:7 NCV

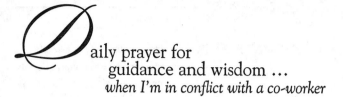

Daily prayer for guidance and wisdom …
when I'm in conflict with a co-worker

> *Don't quarrel with anyone. Be at peace with*
> *everyone, just as much as possible.*
>
> Romans 12:18 TLB

Dear Heavenly Father,

The challenges of managing my class are stressful enough. Now on top of that, one of my own co-workers is giving me a hard time.

Lord, I'm afraid to open my mouth, because I know angry words will probably be the result. That will only make the situation worse. I pray that You will calm my spirit and fill me with Your Spirit. Help me not to see things through a cloud of pride, but keep my motives pure. Let me be a voice of reason, able to articulate my position calmly and clearly. And when I need to admit that I'm wrong, give me Your courage to do so.

Amen.

> *Those who are hot-tempered stir up strife,*
> *but those who are slow to anger calm contention.*
>
> Proverbs 15:18 NRSV

MY PERSONAL PRAYER

The best way to keep people from jumping down your throat is to keep your mouth shut.

Author Unknown

Dear Father:

_____

_____

_____

_____

_____

_____

Amen

Don't hit back; discover beauty in everyone. If you've got it in you, get along with everybody.
Romans 12:17, 18 MSG

Regarding life together and getting along with each other, you don't need me to tell you what to do. You're God-taught in these matters. Just love one another!
1 Thessalonians 4:9 MSG

Daily prayer for guidance and wisdom ...
when I have an unruly class

> *The wise are known for their understanding,*
> *and instruction is appreciated if it's*
> *well presented.*
>
> Proverbs 16:21 NLT

Dear Heavenly Father,

You know that I think my students are great, but sometimes they push me to the breaking point! When that happens, I pray You will give me the strength to hold my temper in check. Help me know which battles are worth fighting and which to let go, and give me the wisdom to know the quickest, most effective way to bring things back under control.

Lord, I want to model for my students a spirit of fairness and self-control. Let me be the example to them of patience and kindness. And when they are at their most unlovable, fill me with Your love for them.

Amen.

> *Those who control their anger have great understanding;*
> *those with a hasty temper will make mistakes.*
> Proverbs 14:29 NLT

MY PERSONAL PRAYER

It is the man who is cool and collected, who is master of his countenance, his voice, his actions, his gestures, of every part, who can work upon others at his pleasure.
Denis Diderot

Dear Father:

_____

_____

_____

_____

_____

_____

Amen

*The Lord disciplines those whom he loves,
and chastises every child whom he accepts.*
Hebrews 12:6 NRSV

*I know, O LORD, that your decisions are fair;
you disciplined me because I needed it.*
Psalm 119:75 NLT

Prayers to Encourage and Comfort the Soul   97

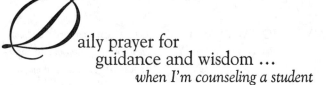

Daily prayer for guidance and wisdom ...
when I'm counseling a student

Let the words of Christ ... live in your hearts
and make you wise. Use his words to teach
and counsel each other.

Colossians 3:16 NLT

Dear Heavenly Father,

You know that, as a teacher, I like to instruct. My job is to share information that will help my students have better lives today and tomorrow. It's hard for me to put aside my teacher role and be a friend, but there are times when my students need me to do just that.

Lord, make me sensitive to those times when I need to listen to my students without offering any advice. I want my students to feel comfortable in sharing with me the things that are on their hearts and minds. Help me respond to them in ways that show how much I care about them, not just as students but as thinking, feeling individuals.

Amen.

Without good direction, people lose their way.
Proverbs 11:14 MSG

MY PERSONAL PRAYER

*Advice is like snow; the softer it
falls, the longer it dwells upon and
the deeper it sinks into the mind.*
Samuel Taylor Coleridge

Dear Father:

_____

_____

_____

_____

_____

_____

Amen

*The Lord GOD hath given me the tongue of the learned,
that I should know how to speak a word
in season to him that is weary.*
Isaiah 50:4 KJV

*I listen carefully to what God the LORD is saying, for he
speaks peace to his people, his faithful ones.*
Psalm 85:8 NLT

Prayers to Encourage and Comfort the Soul   99

*D*aily prayer for
guidance and wisdom ...
when I'm praising a student

> *Jesus said, "If you give even a cup of cold
> water to one of the least of my followers, you
> will surely be rewarded."*
> Matthew 10:42 NLT

Dear Heavenly Father,

Compliments for students' good performances roll so easily off my tongue that I'm afraid the words sometimes lose their meaning. Lord, help me to be as thoughtful and deliberate about the ways I praise my students as I am about the ways I correct them. Give me creative ideas for rewards and praises that are truly meaningful, especially for those students who continually do well.

I also want my students to know without any doubt how proud I am of them—not just when they succeed but also when they try hard. Show me those times when they need to be praised simply for making an effort.

Amen.

> *Withhold not good from them to whom it is due.*
> Proverbs 3:27 KJV

MY PERSONAL PRAYER

Words of praise, indeed, are almost as necessary to warm a child into a congenial life as acts of kindness and affection.
Judicious praise is to children what the sun is to flowers.

Christian Nestell Bovee

Dear Father:

_____

_____

_____

_____

_____

_____

Amen

Render therefore to all their due: ... honor to whom honor.
Romans 13:7 NKJV

A word fitly spoken is like apples of gold in pictures of silver.
Proverbs 25:11 KJV

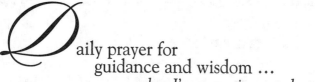

Daily prayer for guidance and wisdom ...

when I'm correcting a student

Withhold not correction from the child.
Proverbs 23:13 KJV

Dear Heavenly Father,

I know the Bible says that You correct Your children because You love us. But I have to admit that, more times than not, I correct my students because I'm angry and frustrated!

Lord, teach me the true intent of correction. When I'm tempted to lash out in anger at my class, remind me that correction without purpose is, at best, meaningless and, at worst, destructive. In those times when my class needs correction, still my spirit, then show me how to respond in a way that will help my students grow in maturity and character. Show me how to follow Your example of correcting in love.

Amen.

*The LORD corrects those he loves,
just as a father corrects a child in whom he delights.*
Proverbs 3:12 NLT

MY PERSONAL PRAYER

*Discipline and love are not
antithetical; one is a function
of the other.*

James Dobson

Dear Father:

_____

_____

_____

_____

_____

_____

Amen

*All discipline seems painful rather than pleasant;
later it yields the peaceful fruit of righteousness to those
who have been trained by it.*
Hebrews 12:11 RSV

*Correct me, LORD, but please be gentle.
Do not correct me in anger, for I would die.*
Jeremiah 10:24 NLT

Prayers to Encourage and Comfort the Soul   103

*D*aily prayer for
guidance and wisdom ...
when I'm dealing with difficult parents

> *Walk in a manner worthy of the calling with*
> *which you have been called, with all humility*
> *and gentleness, with patience, showing for-*
> *bearance to one another in love.*
>
> Ephesians 4:1, 2 NASB

Dear Heavenly Father,

I don't understand parents who consider me "the
enemy," but inevitably, every new class brings parents
who are convinced I am out to see their child fail.
Lord, for these parents, I pray that You would soften
their hearts and give them a spirit of cooperation. Help
them understand how much I care about their children
and want them to do well. Give me ways to reach these
parents, work with them, and resolve their fears.

Most of all, Lord, don't let me put children in the middle of my struggles with their parents. Don't let me ever
take out my frustrations with parents on the children.

Amen.

A gentle answer turns away wrath, but harsh words stir up anger.
Proverbs 15:1 NLT

MY PERSONAL PRAYER *Patience achieves more than force.*
Edmund Burke

Dear Father:

_____

_____

_____

_____

_____

_____

Amen

When she speaks, her words are wise, and kindness is the rule
for everything she says.
Proverbs 31:26 TLB

You must understand this, my beloved: let everyone be quick
to listen, slow to speak, slow to anger.
James 1:19 NRSV

Prayers to Encourage and Comfort the Soul 105

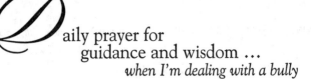

Daily prayer for guidance and wisdom ...
when I'm dealing with a bully

Dear Heavenly Father,

The truth is ... I'm as afraid of bullies as my students are! I'm afraid that if I do anything to stop a bully's aggression, that aggression will be turned on me and, maybe, my family.

Lord, You have said that You have not given us a spirit of fear, but of love. Take away my fear of bullies and give me Your love for them. Give me the courage to stand up for the victims of their rage, and show me how to respond in ways that are both effective and acceptable within our school's policies. I know that Your heart breaks for these damaged children—give me Your heart for them too.

Amen.

MY PERSONAL PRAYER   *A part of kindness consists of loving*
                            people more than they deserve.
                            Joseph Joubert

Dear Father:

_____

_____

_____

_____

_____

_____

_____

                                            Amen

Jesus said, "He pays even greater attention to you ...
even numbering the hairs on your head! So don't be
intimidated by all this bully talk."
Luke 12:7 MSG

Let us try to do what makes peace and helps one another.
Romans 14:19 NCV

Daily prayer for guidance and wisdom …
when a student experiences a family tragedy

He will encourage the fainthearted, those
tempted to despair.

Isaiah 42:3 TLB

Dear Heavenly Father,

When my students hurt, I hurt too. I wish we could keep the world of darkness and tragedy out of our classroom and that everything inside would be nothing but sunshine and happiness. But Lord, even the young hearts of my students are sometimes burdened with adult-sized sorrows.

Let our classroom be a haven of caring and safety for my students when they experience family tragedies. When I feel helpless before their pain, let me radiate a spirit of comfort, and give me the words to say that will ease their suffering. Most of all, when my students come to me with their burdens, let them see You through me.

Amen.

I had fainted, unless I had believed to see the goodness of the LORD
in the land of the living.

Psalm 27:13 KJV

MY PERSONAL PRAYER   *Love is all we have, the only way*
                          that each can help the other.
                                            Euripedes

Dear Father:

———————————————————————————

———————————————————————————

———————————————————————————

———————————————————————————

———————————————————————————

———————————————————————————

———————————————————————————

                                            Amen

The Spirit of the Lord GOD …
has sent Me to heal the brokenhearted.
                    Isaiah 61:1 NKJV

We have great joy and consolation in your love, because the
hearts of the saints have been refreshed by you.
                    Philemon 1:7 NKJV

*D*aily prayer for
guidance and wisdom ...
when I'm balancing my responsibilities

Jesus said, "'You shall love the LORD
your God with all your heart, with all
your soul, with all your mind, and with
all your strength.'"

Mark 12:30 NKJV

Dear Heavenly Father,

If I let it, my job would take over my life! From papers
to grade to after-school sporting events, school duties
are endless. And too often, I find my home life suffering
because of my dedication to being "the best teacher ever."

Lord, remind me of the importance of a balanced life.
Give me the energy to put my whole heart into school
while I'm there, then into my family after the school
day ends. Help me not to over commit to outside activities and to keep You and my family at the center of my
priorities. I am so blessed to have a wonderful job and
home—show me how to give each the attention it
deserves.

Amen.

Making the most of the time, because the days are evil.
Ephesians 5:16 RSV

MY PERSONAL PRAYER

"Holy leisure" refers to a sense of balance in the life, an ability to be at peace through the activities of the day, an ability to rest and take time to enjoy beauty, an ability to pace ourselves.

Richard J. Foster

Dear Father:

_____

_____

_____

_____

_____

_____

Amen

Six days you shall do your work,
and on the seventh day you shall rest.
Exodus 23:12 NKJV

He saw that rest was good.
Genesis 49:15 NKJV

O Lord, support me all the day long,
Until the shadows lengthen,
Until the evening comes,
Until the busy world is hushed,
Until the fever of life is over,
Until my work is done.

J. H. Newman

Daily Prayers for Strength
and Encouragement ...

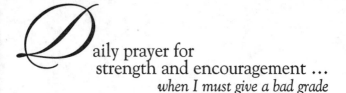

Daily prayer for
strength and encouragement ...
when I must give a bad grade

You teach about the way of God regardless of the consequences. You are impartial and don't play favorites.

Matthew 22:16 NLT

Dear Heavenly Father,

I wonder if my students realize that bad grades are as hard for me to give as they are for them to receive.

Lord, don't let bad grades be a discouragement. Let them be an incentive for my students to work harder to grasp the concepts and skills they need to learn. Also, let bad grades be an incentive for me to examine my teaching methods. Make me aware when the reason my students aren't making good grades is my deficient teaching. Then, help me to humbly admit and correct those deficiencies, keeping my eyes on the goal of helping every one of my students to succeed.

Amen.

Punishment and correction make a child wise.
Proverbs 29:15 NCV

MY PERSONAL PRAYER

Correction does much, but encouragement does more.
Encouragement after censure is as the sun after a shower.
Johann Wolfgang von Goethe

Dear Father:

_____

_____

_____

_____

_____

_____

Amen

Anyone who loves learning accepts being corrected.
Proverbs 12:1 NCV

Take good counsel and accept correction—that's the way to live wisely and well.
Proverbs 19:20 MSG

aily prayer for
strength and encouragement ...
when I'm tempted to lose my temper

Don't be quick to fly off the handle.
Anger boomerangs.

Ecclesiastes 7:9 MSG

Dear Heavenly Father,

Probably the greatest temptation I face on any day is
to fly off the handle! There are so many little aggrava-
tions that build up, and before I know it, I'm an out-
of-control mess.

Lord, I know that as a human being, I'm sometimes
going to lose my temper. When I do, please forgive me
and help me to forgive myself. Then help me to act
quickly to repair any damage that my temper has
caused. Don't let pride get in the way of my apologizing
when I need to. Help me to lay a solid foundation of
trust and mutual respect so that on occasion, when I do
lose my temper, my students' confidence in my love
and care for them won't be shaken.

Amen.

God's righteousness doesn't grow from human anger.
James 1:20 MSG

MY PERSONAL PRAYER

Temper, if ungoverned,
governs the whole man.
Anthony Ashley Cooper Shaftesbury

Dear Father:

_____

_____

_____

_____

_____

_____

Amen

Bad temper is contagious—don't get infected.
Proverbs 22:25 MSG

A person who quickly loses his temper does foolish things. But
a person with understanding remains calm.
Proverbs 14:17 NCV

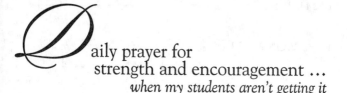

Daily prayer for strength and encouragement ...
when my students aren't getting it

> *Let us not get tired of doing what is right, for*
> *after a while we will reap a harvest of blessing*
> *is we don't get discouraged and give up.*
>
> Galatians 6:9 TLB

Dear Heavenly Father,

There's nothing quite like that feeling in the pit of your stomach when you've put your heart and soul into a lesson, only to look out at a sea of blank stares. When that happens, I fee like a compete failure who never should have become a teacher in the first place!

Lord, for those times when a lesson bombs, I pray for Your perspective—it's one lesson, not the end of the world. I pray that You would give me the wisdom to know where and how things went wrong and the encouragement to take myself a little more lightly.

Amen.

> *Be strong and brave. Don't be afraid or discouraged.*
> 1 Chronicles 22:13 NCV

MY PERSONAL PRAYER

It is with many enterprises as with striking fire; we do not meet with success except by reiterated efforts, and often at the instant when we despaired of success.

Madam de Maintenon

Dear Father:

_____

_____

_____

_____

_____

_____

Amen

We are pressed on every side by troubles, but we are not crushed and broken. We are perplexed, but we don't give up and quit.
2 Corinthians 4:8 NLT

Take charge! Take heart! Don't be anxious or get discouraged. GOD, my God, is with you in this; he won't walk off and leave you in the lurch. He's at your side.
1 Chronicles 28:20 MSG

Daily prayer for strength and encouragement ...
when I have an opportunity to share my faith

> *Many people will praise God because you follow the Good News of Christ—the gospel you say you believe—and because you freely share with them and with all others.*
>
> 2 Corinthians 9:13 NCV

Dear Heavenly Father,

There are so many nitpicky rules and regulations about the "separation of church and state" that I feel any expression of my faith is completely unwelcome at school. But there are so many times when I feel Your Spirit nudge me to say something that will point others to You.

Lord, help me to clearly discern Your voice about when to share my faith. And when You tell me to do so, give me the strength to speak out with confidence and love. Protect me from any retaliation against my standing up for You, and give me the words and actions that will bring the greatest honor to Your name.

Amen.

I rejoice and share my joy.
Philippians 2:17 NASB

MY PERSONAL PRAYER

*Being an extrovert isn't essential
to evangelism—
obedience and love are.*
Rebecca Manley Pippert

Dear Father:

_____

_____

_____

_____

_____

_____

_____

Amen

*I pray that as you share your faith with others it will grip their
lives too, as they see the wealth of good things in you that
come from Christ Jesus.*
Philemon 1:6 TLB

*Be wise in the way you act with people who are not believers.
Use your time in the best way you can.*
Colossians 4:5 NCV

Daily prayer for strength and encouragement ...
when I receive criticism from my superiors

> *If you profit from constructive criticism, you will be elected to the wise men's hall of fame. But to reject criticism is to harm yourself and your own best interests.*
>
> Proverbs 15:31, 32 TLB

Dear Heavenly Father,

I guess it's just human nature to be defensive in receiving criticism. I certainly am!

Lord, I need an attitude adjustment toward criticism. Help me to be grateful when my principal and other supervisors care enough about my success as a teacher to give me constructive criticism. Don't let pride cloud my response, but help me to learn from them how to be more effective. After all, what I really want is to be the very best I can be for the sake of my students, and if my superiors can help me achieve that goal through their thoughtful criticism, let me receive it with an open heart.

Amen.

Poverty and shame will come to him who disdains correction, but he who regards a rebuke will be honored.
Proverbs 13:18 NKJV

MY PERSONAL PRAYER

To avoid criticism, do nothing,
say nothing, be nothing.
Elbert Green Hubbard

Dear Father:

_____

_____

_____

_____

_____

_____

Amen

The road to life is a disciplined life; ignore correction
and you're lost for good.
Proverbs 10:17 MSG

Whoever learns from correction is wise.
Proverbs 15:5 NLT

Prayers to Encourage and Comfort the Soul　　123

*D*aily prayer for
strength and encouragement ...
when I'm tempted to gossip

> *Though some tongues just love the taste of gossip, Christians have better uses for language ... That kind of talk doesn't fit our style.*
>
> Ephesians 5:4 MSG

Dear Heavenly Father,

Gossip is such an easy trap to fall into. Too often I find myself in the middle of a gossip session before I'm even aware of it! Lord, I know why Your Word so clearly condemns gossip—I've seen it undermine honest efforts and destroy relationships in our own school.

Lord, forgive me for those times when I've gossiped about others. Help me to walk away from the situations that lead to gossip and resist even the strongest temptation to participate. I want my interactions with others to be honoring to You. Let me be an example of how You would have us treat each other.

Amen.

Without wood, a fire will go out, and without gossip, quarreling will stop.
Proverbs 26:20 NCV

MY PERSONAL PRAYER

Never believe anything bad about anybody unless you positively know it to be true; never tell even that unless you feel that it is absolutely necessary—and remember that God is listening while you tell it.

Henry Van Dyke

Dear Father:

_____

_____

_____

_____

_____

_____

Amen

A person who gossips ruins friendships.
Proverbs 16:28 NCV

A gossip goes around revealing secrets, but those who are trustworthy can keep a confidence.
Proverbs 11:13 NLT

Daily prayer for strength and encouragement ...
when I'm tired

God gives power to those who are tired and worn out; he offers strength to the weak.
Isaiah 40:29 NLT

Dear Heavenly Father,

There are days when I feel that I just can't keep up the frantic pace of my life anymore. Everyone expects so much from me. Between the requirements of my job and the demands on me outside the classroom, I'm exhausted.

Lord, I come to You asking for Your renewal and strength for each part of my life. Teach me to always take the time to be still before You and drink directly from Your overflowing fount of refreshment. Lord, I cast all my cares on You with the confidence that You have promised to meet each and every one of my needs. Thank You for loving and caring for me!

Amen.

Take a new grip with your tired hands and stand firm on your shaky legs.
Hebrews 12:12 NLT

MY PERSONAL PRAYER

Rest is the sweet sauce of labor.
Plutarch

Dear Father:

_____

_____

_____

_____

_____

_____

Amen

The sun of righteousness will dawn on those who honor my name, healing radiating from its wings. You will be bursting with energy, like colts frisky and frolicking.
Malachi 4:2 MSG

My grace is sufficient for you, for My strength is made perfect in weakness.
2 Corinthians 12:9 NKJV

Prayers to Encourage and Comfort the Soul

Daily prayer for strength and encouragement ...
when I'm feeling insecure

Be my strong refuge, to which I may
resort continually.

Psalm 71:3 NKJV

Dear Heavenly Father,

My students have complete faith in me. They expect me to know everything, to have the answers to all their questions. If they only knew how much I worry about letting them down!

Lord, sometimes I feel so insecure about my ability to meet the challenges of teaching. I also try to present an air of confidence, but sometimes I feel like a fraud. At those times, teach me to turn to You. I know that You understand my insecurities and weaknesses, and You want to use them to show Your glory and strength. Lord, give me true confidence, not in my abilities but in Your promise to guide me and provide the resources I need to do a good job.

Amen.

Be strong in the Lord, and in the power of His might.
Ephesians 6:10 NKJV

MY PERSONAL PRAYER

*God wants us to be victors, not
victims; to grow, not grovel;
to soar, not sink; to overcome,
not to be overwhelmed.*
William Arthur Ward

Dear Father:

_____

_____

_____

_____

_____

_____

Amen

*The LORD is my rock, and my fortress, and my deliverer;
my God, my strength, in whom I will trust.*
Psalm 18:2 KJV

*You are safe in the care of the LORD your God,
secure in his treasure pouch!*
1 Samuel 25:29 NLT

aily prayer for
strength and encouragement ...
when a student drops out of school

Lord, listen to my words.
Understand what I am thinking.

Psalm 5:1 NCV

Dear Heavenly Father,

It's hard to see a student fail. But to see one deliberately choose to abandon school is devastating. Lord, when students leave school by choice, I pray that You would go with them. Protect them and guide them as they face the world without the education they need to truly succeed. Impress on them the need to return to school, and give them the courage to do so.

Also, Lord, if there's any way that I've contributed to a student's dropping out, please make it very clear to me. Then, help me to accept responsibility with humility and make any needed changes so that every student that I teach will be inspired to strive for the goal of finishing school.

Amen.

The Lord God says, "Anyone who trusts in me will not be disappointed."
Isaiah 49:23 NCV

MY PERSONAL PRAYER

All I have seen teaches me to trust
the Creator for all I have not seen.
Ralph Waldo Emerson

Dear Father:

_____

_____

_____

_____

_____

_____

Amen

You are my hope, O Lord GOD;
You are my trust from my youth.
Psalm 71:5 NKJV

It is good for me to draw near to God: I have put my trust in
the Lord GOD, that I may declare all Your works.
Psalm 73:28 NKJV

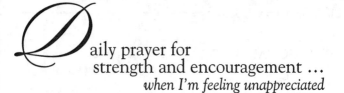

Daily prayer for strength and encouragement ...
when I'm feeling unappreciated

How precious it is, Lord, to realize that you
are thinking about me constantly!
Psalm 139:17 TLB

Dear Heavenly Father,

Here I am again—feeling sorry for myself. Nobody could possibly work harder than I do or pour more heart and soul into a job than I do. Yet recognition for a job well done is so hard to come by around here, while criticism is commonplace.

Lord, I know that Your Word says I should work for You, not for human rewards. Help me to remember that my worth as a teacher is not based on praise from others, and bless me with Your approval of my work. Remind my heart that even when no one else notices all the good things I do, You do, and that's enough.

Amen.

God, my strength, I will sing praises to you ...
you are the God who loves me.
Psalm 59:17 NCV

MY PERSONAL PRAYER

It feels good to be appreciated,
but the sheer enjoyment of
the sun on your face ...
and the giggle of a baby gives
true meaning to the world.

Greg Henry Quinn

Dear Father:

_____

_____

_____

_____

_____

_____

Amen

The LORD does not see as man sees; for man looks at the
outward appearance, but the LORD looks at the heart."
1 Samuel 16:7 NKJV

Jesus said, "The Father himself loves you. He loves
you because you have loved me and believed that
I came from God."
John 16:27 NCV

Prayers to Encourage and Comfort the Soul   133

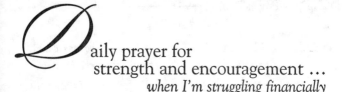

Daily prayer for strength and encouragement …

when I'm struggling financially

> *Jesus said, "The Father will give you all you*
> *need from day to day if you make the*
> *Kingdom of God your primary concern."*
>
> Luke 12:31 NLT

Dear Heavenly Father,

You know I didn't become a teacher to strike it rich. I chose this profession believing that some things are more important than money. But these days, my idealism is overshadowed by bills and unexpected financial demands. And I have to admit, I often wish I had chosen a different, more lucrative profession!

Lord, I believe in my heart that You meant for me to be a teacher. Help me also to believe that You will provide for all my financial needs. Let me rest in the knowledge that I am following Your will for my life and that You will always give me "my daily bread."

Amen.

> *Happy are those who fear the LORD.*
> *They confidently trust the LORD to care for them.*
>
> Psalm 112:1, 7 NLT

MY PERSONAL PRAYER

He who gives us teeth
will give us bread.
Jewish Proverb

Dear Father:

_____

_____

_____

_____

_____

_____

Amen

God will provide rain for the seeds you sow. The grain that grows will be
abundant. Your cattle will range far and wide.
Isaiah 30:23 MSG

Jesus said, "Don't worry about food—what to eat and drink. Don't
worry whether God will provide it for you. These things dominate the
thoughts of most people, but your Father already knows your needs."
Luke 12:29, 30 NLT

*D*aily prayer for
strength and encouragement ...
when I'm feeling burned out

> *Jesus said, "Take My yoke upon you and
> learn from Me, for I am gentle and lowly in
> heart, and you will find rest for your souls.."*
> Matthew 11:29 NKJV

Dear Heavenly Father,

More often than not, the reality of teaching is a far cry
from my expectations, and I find myself daydreaming
about getting in my car and driving away from school,
never to return.

Lord, help me deal with the realities of teaching. Keep
my expectations in check, and don't let the disappoint-
ments overwhelm me. Remind me of the things I love
about teaching, and give me the peace to accept those
realities that I can't change. Keep me optimistic and
focused on the positives. And renew my enthusiasm
and energy for the privilege of leading students on the
path of learning.

Amen.

> *This is the time and place to rest. This is the place
> to lay down your burden.*
> Isaiah 28:12 MSG

MY PERSONAL PRAYER

Our greatest danger in life is in permitting the urgent things to crowd out the important.

Charles E. Hummel

Dear Father:

_____

_____

_____

_____

_____

_____

Amen

Jesus said, "Come to Me, all who are weary and heavy-laden, and I will give you rest."
Matthew 11:28 NASB

May the God of hope fill you up with joy, fill you up with peace, so that your believing lives, filled with the life-giving energy of the Holy Spirit, will brim over with hope!
Romans 15:13 MSG

Prayers to Encourage and Comfort the Soul   137

Daily prayer for strength and encouragement …
when I'm feeling like a failure

Lord our God, be pleased with us. Give us success in what we do.

Psalm 90:17 NCV

Dear Heavenly Father,

I blew it—again. Sometimes I think I'm destined to fail, no matter how hard I try, no matter how much I want to succeed.

Lord, thank You for never giving up on me or considering me a failure. I know that even though I'm not perfect, You are and that it's only through You living in me that I can ever do anything worthwhile. Teach me to turn every day over to You. I want You to accomplish Your purpose through me, Lord. And when I feel like a failure, remind me that You still love me and have a valuable part for me to play in Your work.

Amen.

Remember the Lord in everything you do. And he will give you success.
Proverbs 3:6 NCV

MY PERSONAL PRAYER

*One cannot know the true sweet-
ness of success without having
experienced the pain of failure.*
Author Unknown

Dear Father:

_____

_____

_____

_____

_____

_____

Amen

*Lord, all our success is because of what you have done.
So give us peace.*
Isaiah 26:12 NCV

*May the LORD be with you and give you success as
you follow his instructions.*
1 Chronicles 22:11 NLT

A Prayer of Thankfulness

Thou hast given so much to me,
Give one thing more—a grateful heart;
Not thankful when it pleaseth me,
As if thy blessings had spare days,
But such a heart whose Pulse may be
Thy Praise.

George Herbert

Daily Prayers of Thankfulness …

*D*aily prayer of gratitude ...
when I receive a favorable evaluation

> *The light of the eyes rejoices the heart, and a*
> *good report makes the bones healthy.*
>
> Proverbs 15:30 NKJV

Dear Heavenly Father,

My heart overflows with praise to You when I am rewarded with a positive evaluation. I want to shout "Hallelujah!" and go skipping down the school halls.

Lord, thank You when I receive recognition for my work from those in authority over me. Their approval is so important, and I work tirelessly to hear them say "Good job!" But I pray that pleasing my earthly bosses would never become more important to me than pleasing You. Make me worthy of heavenly commendations too. Help me always strive to receive the ultimate positive evaluation from You—the words "Well done, good and faithful servant."

Amen.

A good reputation is more valuable than the most expensive perfume.
Ecclesiastes 7:1 NLT

MY PERSONAL PRAYER

Excellence is the bull's eye.
Author Unknown

Dear Father:

_____

_____

_____

_____

_____

_____

Amen

Success to you. Success to those who help you,
because your God helps you.
1 Chronicles 12:18 NCV

His lord said unto him, 'Well done, good and faithful servant;
you have been faithful over a few things, I will make you
ruler over many things.'
Matthew 25:23 NKJV

Prayers to Encourage and Comfort the Soul   143

*D*aily prayer of gratitude ...
when I see a student improve

*We are glad when we are weak and you
are strong. What we pray for is
your improvement.*

2 Corinthians 13:9 RSV

Dear Heavenly Father,

I live for those golden moments, those times when all the hard work pays off and students make a noticeable improvement. I love seeing the pride of accomplishment reflected in students' eyes, and I can't help but feel that I've made a difference that matters!

Lord, thank You for those times. Help me to be grateful and not puffed up, remembering to give You the glory. Let each little step of improvement be one of many to come for my students. Every day, give me the wisdom to guide them toward success, and help me to serve my students with unwavering excellence and dedication.

Amen.

*Jesus said, "I chose you and appointed you that you should go and bear
fruit, and that your fruit should remain."*
John 15:16 KJV

MY PERSONAL PRAYER

A student's success in school starts in the heads and hearts of his or her parents and teachers. The way we see them, the way they see themselves, is what they will become.

Linda Holt,
1995 Hawaii Teacher of the Year

Dear Father:

_____

_____

_____

_____

_____

_____

Amen

I will instruct you (says the Lord) and guide you along the best pathway for your life; I will advise you and watch your progress.
Psalm 32:8 TLB

Jesus said, "I know all the things you do—your love, your faith, your service, and your patient endurance. And I can see your constant improvement in all these things."
Revelation 2:19 NLT

Prayers to Encourage and Comfort the Soul   145

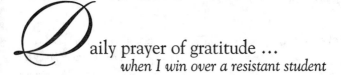

Daily prayer of gratitude ...
when I win over a resistant student

*Be patient and you will finally win, for a soft
tongue can break hard bones.*

Proverbs 25:15 TLB

Dear Heavenly Father,

Thank You for those times when You melt hearts that
seem to be made of stone. It's hard to keep trying to
break through a student's wall of resistance. I often feel
like I'm just banging my head against that wall. But
then, when there's finally a crack and a glimmer of
light shines through, it's worth all the effort and pain.

Lord, make me a stubborn person. Never allow me to
give up on any student. And on those occasions when
I'm tempted to do so, give me the strength to perse-
vere. I'm grateful that I can rely on You to work in the
hearts of my students—even the resistant ones.

Amen.

From a wise mind comes careful and persuasive speech.
Proverbs 16:23 TLB

MY PERSONAL PRAYER   *Not all people can be driven by the*
same stick.

Arabian Proverb

Dear Father:

_____

_____

_____

_____

_____

_____

Amen

It is not that we think we can do anything of lasting value by
ourselves. Our only power and success come from God.
2 Corinthians 3:5 NLT

It's not possible for a person to succeed—I'm talking about
eternal success without—heaven's help.
John 3:27 MSG

*D*aily prayer of gratitude ...
when I see my students graduate

I am filled with joy at his success.

John 3:29 NLT

Dear Heavenly Father,

My soul breathes a sigh of relief when my students graduate! Your faithfulness in bringing them to this important milestone in life brings me to tears. Of course, for some, the process has been a breeze. I pray that You would continue their success beyond graduation. And for those who have struggled to get to this point, I pray for a special outpouring of Your love and blessing.

Most importantly, Lord, help each of these students find You. I pray that during the short time I have been in their lives, I have been able to plant a seed in their hearts that will bloom into a lasting, life-changing faith.

Amen.

Let us run with patience the particular race that God has set before us. Keep your eyes on Jesus, our leader and instructor.

Hebrews 12:1, 2 TLB

MY PERSONAL PRAYER

My greatest satisfaction comes when my students find the success they never thought they could have.
Addie Rhodes Lee

Dear Father:

_____

_____

_____

_____

_____

_____

Amen

You need to stick it out, staying with God's plan so you'll be there for the promised completion.
Hebrews 10:36 MSG

I have fought a good fight, I have finished my course, I have kept the faith.
2 Timothy 4:7 KJV

*D*aily prayer of gratitude ...
when my efforts are recognized

> *You're blessed when you meet Lady Wisdom,*
> *when you make friends with Madame Insight*
> *... With one hand she gives long life, with the*
> *other she confers recognition.*
>
> Proverbs 3:13, 16 MSG

Dear Heavenly Father,

Thank You for those times when my efforts receive recognition from others. Even small acknowledgements of my work go a long way in boosting my perseverance for a job that is tough and often thankless.

And for those times when my perseverance runs thin and I begin to wonder if my efforts are in vain, renew my commitment to my profession. Give me the confidence that I am where You have called me to be.

Lord, I want to honor You in everything I do. Thank You for all the little ways that You impress on my heart Your recognition of, and blessing on, the work of my hands.

Amen.

A woman who fears the LORD, she shall be praised. Give her of the
fruit of her hands, and let her own works praise her in the gates.
Proverbs 31:30, 31 NKJV

MY PERSONAL PRAYER

*Be satisfied with nothing
but your best.*
Edward Rowland Sill

Dear Father:

_____

_____

_____

_____

_____

_____

Amen

Recognition comes from God, not legalistic critics.
Romans 2:29 MSG

My soul shall make her boast in the LORD.
Psalm 34:2 KJV

*D*aily prayer of gratitude ...
when I receive unexpected encouragement

> *Anxious hearts are very heavy, but a word of*
> *encouragement does wonders!*
>
> Proverbs 12:25 TLB

Dear Heavenly Father,

Thank You for knowing when I need an extra little "lift" in my day. An unexpected note from a parent, a pat on the back from my principal—I'm constantly amazed at how You bring encouragement into my life at just the right time, just when I need it most.

Lord, thank You for bringing other people into my life to show me Your love.

Help me to be a source of Your love and encouragement to them too. Show me others who also need a "lift" in their day, then give me the right words to encourage them for You. Please show them Your love through me.

Amen.

> *God loved us. Through his grace he gave us a good hope and*
> *encouragement that continues forever.*
>
> 2 Thessalonians 2:17 NCV

MY PERSONAL PRAYER

*Encouragement is oxygen
to the soul.*
George M. Adams

Dear Father:

_____

_____

_____

_____

_____

_____

Amen

Patience and encouragement come from God.
Romans 15:5 NCV

Encourage each other every day.
Hebrews 3:13 NCV

Topical Reference Index

Teaching is a partnership with God.
You are not molding iron nor chiseling
marble; you are working with the Creator
of the universe in shaping human
character and determining destiny.

Ruth Vaughn

A Teacher's Prayer

God, give me sympathy and sense,
And help me keep my courage high;
God, give me calm and confidence,
And—please—a twinkle in my eye.
Amen.

Margaret Bailey